D0411953

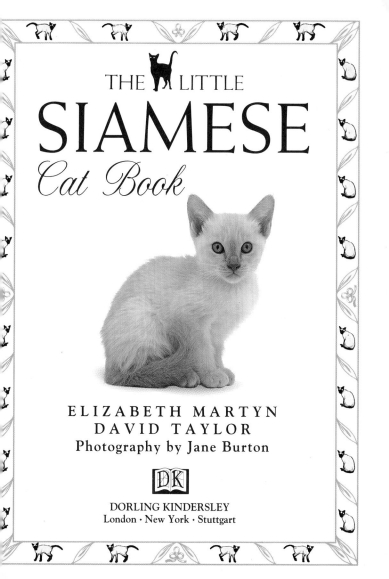

THE LITTLE
SIAMESE
Cat Book

ELIZABETH MARTYN
DAVID TAYLOR
Photography by Jane Burton

DK

DORLING KINDERSLEY
London · New York · Stuttgart

A DORLING KINDERSLEY BOOK

PROJECT EDITOR *Alison Melvin*

ART EDITOR *Lee Griffiths*

MANAGING EDITOR *Krystyna Mayer*

MANAGING ART EDITOR *Derek Coombes*

PRODUCTION *Hilary Stephens*

*First published in Great Britain in 1991 by
Dorling Kindersley Limited, 9 Henrietta Street, London WC2E 8PS*

*A CIP catalogue record for this book is available
from the British Library*

ISBN 0-86318-666-1

*Reproduced by Colourscan, Singapore
Printed and bound in Hong Kong by Imago*

CONTENTS

ORIENTAL
Cat

The prestigious history and ancient origins of the Siamese cat, and its role in the myth and folklore of the Orient.

EASTERN ORIGINS

The earliest known records of Siamese cats date back
to the fourteenth century.

No one seems sure where
Siamese cats came from
originally. Some people say that
they were first found in Siam
(now Thailand),
others believe
that this ancient
and noble breed
of cat originated
in China.

FIRST SIAMESE
Siamese cats were
not seen in the
West until the
late nineteenth
century when the
first cats, named
Pho and Mia,
were sent to the
British Consul
General by the
King of Siam. The British
public caught its first glimpse
of Siamese cats at the Crystal
Palace Cat Show in London in
1885, where Pho and Mia's
kittens were among the prize-
winners. The Siamese cat

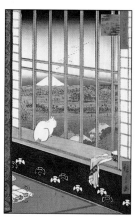

reached America several years
later, when Lockhaven Siam
and Lockhaven Sally Ward
were registered in Chicago. But
the breed proved
delicate at first
and the kittens
frequently died of
Feline Enteritis
until the Orient
cat became better
established.

PERFECT POINTS
The original
Siamese cats to
be brought out of
Thailand were
Seal-points, with
a characteristic
cream-coloured
coat and seal-
brown markings on face, tail,
and paws. The first Blue-point,
with a bluish tinge to the coat
and slate-grey markings, came
to England in the 1890s, while
the lighter-coloured Chocolate-
points arrived in about 1900.

...ft: 19th-
...ntury
...odblock
...t cat
...ght:
...panese
...eping cat
...low:
...itch cats
...Okabe

...terbreeding between Siamese
...different colours has resulted
...a range of point colours,
...cluding lilac, seal, cream,
...bby, and red.

...ARK SIAMESE

...he Birman looks like a
...nghaired Siamese and,
...though it was introduced to
...rope in the 1920s, it was not
...anted recognition until the
...)60s. The Burmese breed
...iginated in America in the
...)30s from a cat called Wong
...au, brought from Burma and
...ossbred with a Siamese cat.

11

ORIENTAL LEGEND

Siamese cats are surrounded by myths. Many of these
stories concern the sacred cats of the Orient.

In ancient times, Siamese cats
had a very important function
as guards of the Buddhist
temples. Their job was to chase
away and even
attack thieves
who attempted
to steal treasure
from the temple.

SACRED CATS
The temple cats
were regarded as
sacred since they
were thought to
enshrine the
souls of the dead.
They were kept
only by priests
and royalty, and
anyone caught
trying to steal a Siamese cat
would be punished by death.
No wonder that these cats were
unknown in the West for so
long. The first Siamese cats,
brought to Europe in the 1880s,
had squinting eyes and kinked
tails, characteristics that have

almost completely disappeared
as a result of very careful
breeding. Elaborate stories were
often told to account for some
of the early
genetic defect
in the breed.

ORIENTAL
LEGENDS
According to
the legend, the
Siamese cat
developed its
squint by gazing
so long and hard
at the treasure
that it guarded.
The kink in its
tail is said to
have come from
its habit of curling around the
treasure at night to protect it
from thieves. Another story
relates how a Siamese princess,
when bathing, would slip her
rings on to her cat's tail, and
would kink the end to keep
them from being lost or stolen.

Left: Detail of silk painting, Cat and Sparrows
Above: Kitten with butterfly
Right: Temple guard

TEMPLE CATS

In Burma, the longhaired Birman was also kept as a sacred temple cat. All Birmans are said to be descended from the pure white cat, Sinh the Oracle, who resided in the Temple of Lao Tsun where the cats were worshipped as gods. The story has it that during an attack on the temple, Sinh leapt to the defence of his master, the high priest Mun-Ha, and was transformed. Immediately his fur took on a golden tinge, his amber eyes turned sapphire-blue and, where his paws touched the dying priest, the fur remained purest white. All Birmans have kept this colouring ever since as a result of Sinh's bravery.

HALL OF FELINE FAME

Siamese and Burmese cats have often been the choice of celebrated owners.

The aristocratic appeal of Siamese cats, with their talkative and intelligent personalities, has endeared them to many famous people since the first cats were brought from the Orient in the 1880s.

STAR STATUS

James Mason and his wife were great cat lovers and always had one or more Siamese around the house. Mason liked to sketch the cats, and even wrote a book about them. When he sailed from London to New York, the cats went too. They spent the journey in Mason's stateroom, but suffered badly from seasickness and spent the entire crossing confined to

their basket. Vivien Leigh was also accompanied on a voyage to Europe by her Siamese cat, Poo Jones, who lived with the star in her Hollywood home. The two sailed on the *Queen Elizabeth* to England in 1960 and Poo Jones took a daily stroll around the deck with his mistress. Renowned for his beautiful violet eyes, Poo Jones was a faithful companion, who stayed close to Vivien Leigh during her last illness and was by her bedside when she died in 1967.

SIAMESE ON CELLULOID

One Siamese cat who became film star in his own right was the feline "actor" who played

*ft: Prince and Princess Michael
Kent, plus pet Siamese
bove: Milk-drinking Siamese
stages a starlet*

...o in the film of Sheila
...rnford's story, *The Incredible
...urney*. The Disney film told
...e story of the intrepid
...amese and two canine
...mpanions, who trekked 300
...iles across the north-western
...lds of Canada to find their
...ay home. A couple of

unforgettable singing Siamese
also featured in the Disney film
Lady and the Tramp. Their
rendering of the song "We are
Siamese" seems to sum up the
Siamese personality.

REGAL CONNECTIONS

Siamese cats feel perfectly at
home in aristocratic company.
Princess Michael of Kent has
even issued official portraits of
herself accompanied by her
Siamese and Burmese cats.

GALLERY
OF SIAMESE
(& NEARLY
SIAMESE)

Cats

*The true aristocrats of the
feline world, from the
sleekest Siamese to the most
adorable Birman.*

FELINE FEATURES

The Oriental breeding of these pedigree cats shows
in their high cheekboned, wedge-shaped faces.
In longhaired types, the face may be softer and
more rounded. The glorious eyes, most usually forget-
me-not blue, are the most striking feature.

Burmese

Birman

Siamese

Colourpoint Longhair

Snowshoe

Tonkinese

Oriental Shorthair

Balinese

SIAMESE

The best-known breed of pedigree cat, the
Siamese is appreciated all over the world.
Today's pure-bred Siamese cat bears little
resemblance to the first cats brought out of Thailand
in the 1880s. Those Victorian cats had thickset, round
heads, squinting eyes, and kinked tails. Systematic
breeding, using only the most elegant and fine-boned
cats, has eliminated these faults, producing the super,
eye-catching felines that
now appear at cat
shows. Apart from
its obvious visual
appeal, the Siamese
also has a distinct
character; although
sometimes a little
aloof, it does form a
close bond with its
owner and is an
affectionate pet.

POINTED OUT
*The Seal-point is genetically a black cat,
but with colour appearing only on the points.*

20

CATERISTICS

Oriental, wedge-shaped head with large ears

A loud voice and loads of energy

An extrovert cat with a very strong personality

BLUE-EYED BOY

All types of Siamese have one thing in common: their beguiling blue eyes.

SLENDER BUILD

The Siamese has long, slim legs with delicate paws, on which it moves with deft grace.

COLOURPOINT LONGHAIR

This adorable cat brings together the best features of two breeds: the subtle colouring of a Siamese and the strokable, silky fur of a pedigree Longhair. Years of careful crossbreeding between Siamese and Longhairs have been needed to produce the creamy coat with dark points on face, ears, legs, and tail. The Colourpoint is a cat with a lot of character, being more lively than most other Longhairs.

FEATHERY TAIL
The tail is short, but what it lacks in length it makes up for with soft plumes of dark fur along its length. Tufts of fur on the toes are another of this cat's characteristics.

CATERISTICS

Saucer-like eyes in brightest sapphire

Luxurious, silky fur

Gentle and loving, but with plenty of Siamese spirit

SELECTIVE BREEDING
Colourpoint Longhairs are bred in many different colours. The Seal Tabby-point is one of the most recent varieties to be recognized.

LUXURIOUS COAT
Although this cat has the markings of a shorthaired Siamese, its body shape is inherited from a Longhair. It is sturdy and stocky, with short legs and a round, wide face; full, fluffy cheeks, and a short, almost snubbed, nose.

BURMESE

Although related to the Siamese, Burmese cats have glossy coats of a uniform colour, with no distinctive point markings. The bod shape is different too, being more muscular and heavier than that of the Siamese. The hind legs are a little shorter than the forelegs, while the face, although wedge-shaped, is more rounded and not as elongated as that of the Siamese. The Burmese is less vocal than its close relative, but it shares the same love of people. It is a sociable breed and is easy-going and tolerant with children, making it an excellent and affectionate family pet.

BROWN BEAUTY
The satin-like coat shows off the rich sable-brown colour t perfection. Brown was the original coat colour of the Burmese. The breed was firs introduced from Burma to San Francisco in the 1930s, as a "dark Siamese".

CATERISTICS

Fond of people; likes
plenty of company

High sheen on the fur,
which is dense and short

Slightly slanting eyes of
glistening gold

RIGHT EYES

All Burmese have arresting
golden eyes, the clearer and
brighter the better.

LUSCIOUS LILAC

The creamy colouring
of the Lilac Burmese is
thoroughly appealing.

BIRMAN

In a class of its own, the Birman has markings rather like those of a Siamese, but all four paws are white. On the hind feet, these white "mittens" should extend up the back of the legs in a series of pointed spurs. One great attraction of the Birman is its easy-care coat which, although of medium length, does not matt and requires only light brushing to keep it immaculate.

SACRED CATS
The Birman became a recognized breed in America in 1967, a year after Britain. It is sometimes known as the "holy" or "sacred" cat because of its origins around the temples of Burma.

CATERISTICS

White mittens
a all four feet

dapts well to
ther animals

oat does not
need much
grooming

LIVELY CHARACTER

The Birman has a longer
body and narrower face
than most other
longhaired cats,
although it is not as
lithe as a Siamese.
It has a lively
and cheeky
personality.

LUE EYES, DARK FACE

brant blue eyes set in a
't, dark face make a
nning effect. The
es are round, with a
ght upward slant at
e outer corners. The
at is fine and soft.

SNOWSHOE

The Snowshoe breed was developed in America and is still something of a rarity. It originated from three white-pawed kittens, born to Siamese parents. These were used to start a breeding programme and, once the type was established, American Bicoloured Shorthair cats were used to develop it further. The cat has point markings and a short, glossy coat like a Siamese, and the dainty white paws that are typical of a Birman.

NOBLE FEATURES
This aristocratic breed of cat has a noble face with high cheekbones, slanting blue eyes and wide-set ears.

SILVER MITTENS
The Blue-point Snowshoe has a creamy white body with paler chest and tummy and dark greyish-blue points. The cat is also bred as a Seal-point, which has a medium-brown body, darker points, and white paws.

SLEEK SILHOUETTE

The Snowshoe is a medium-sized cat, bigger and heavier than the Siamese, but with a lithe and athletic body. Its fur is sleek with a good, glossy shine.

CATERISTICS

Pure white paws

Sparkling blue eyes

Not at all nervy;
loves being shown

29

TONKINESE

Developed in America and not yet fully recognized in Britain, the Tonkinese is a cross between a Siamese and a Burmese. The breed has many attractive characteristics. "Tonks" are extremely friendly and affectionate and love being cuddled. They are handsome cats, slightly sturdier than the Siamese, and their coats are as soft and sumptuous to the touch as mink.

Slanty Eyes
There's no mistaking the Oriental influence in the face of the Tonkinese. The wedge-shaped head, large, pointed ears, and slanting, blue-green eyes give the game away.

CHARACTERISTICS

Pleasant, outgoing character. Very keen on people

Fur has a natural sheen and feels just like mink

Long, tapering tail

PURE-BRED "TONKS"
Tonkinese can present a problem for breeders, since when two similar Tonkinese are mated, only half the resulting litter of kittens is likely to be true to the breed.

COLOUR VARIETIES
The Red-point Tonkinese was first bred in Britain. The colours of the coat take several months to develop fully.

Foreign Shorthair

The Foreign or Oriental Shorthair, in all it myriad variations, is the result of breeding Siamese cats with other shorthaired cats. This cat has a uniform coat colour with no point markings, but it has all the elegance and distinction the Siamese-type body and face, as well as its endearing and lively personality. The breed was recognized in the late 1970s and there are more than 30 colour varieties, ranging from black, white, and red, to tabby and tortoiseshell.

ELEGANT PROFILE
The Foreign Blue boasts a coat of dark grey with a distinct bluish tinge. A sleek svelte creature, it has ultra-fine, smooth-textured fur that lies very flat. The body is lithe and slim, with long, slender legs, and is offset by a lean tail that tapers down to a fine point.

EMERALD GREEN EYES
Foreign Shorthairs differ from Siamese, not only in their lack of points, but also in the colour of their eyes. Most varieties have vivid green eyes, although for some colour types, eyes of amber, dark orange, copper, or sapphire-blue are permissible.

ORIENTAL TABBY

This is no common or garden tabby, but an Oriental Chocolate Tabby Shorthair. The typical tabby swirls and stripes show up to perfection on its athletic body. The pointed face and large ears indicate its Siamese blood.

CATERISTICS

*

Much like the Siamese in shape

*

Alert and curious

*

People-lovers that make good pets

BALINESE

Sink your fingers into his silken fur, and the friendly Balinese won't mind a bit. These cats are highly affectionate and adore lots of attention. They are thought to have originated as a longhaired variation of the Siamese, and are now bred in their own right. They have the same markings and lean body shape as the Siamese, but have slightly less extrovert personalities. With their glamorous looks and loving natures, they make perfect feline companions.

*B*IG SOFTY
The Balinese coat is delightfully soft and strokable. The fur is shorter than that of most types of longhaired cat, and may even have a slight wave.

FAMILY PLAY

Female Balinese make good mothers, producing adorably fluffy kittens with whom they love to play. In fact, the Balinese always enjoys a game, either with other cats or with its owners.

CHARACTERISTICS

* Same coat colouring and markings as the Siamese

* Glorious, almond-shaped, vivid blue eyes

* A charming personality that loves people

SUBTLE COLOURING

The Lilac Tabby-point Balinese has a creamy white body, with point markings on paws, face, and tail of a discreet greyish-lilac. In America, this variety is called the Frost Lynx-point. The relatively tangle-free coat benefits from grooming every day.

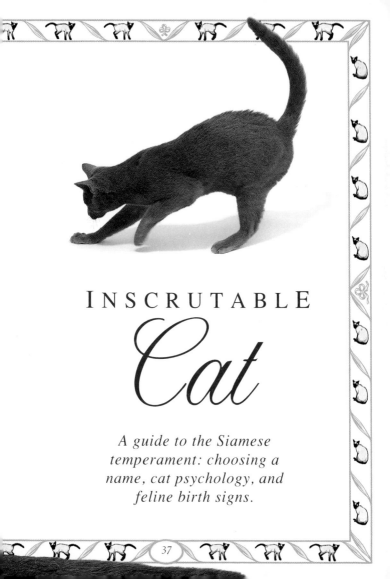

INSCRUTABLE
Cat

*A guide to the Siamese
temperament: choosing a
name, cat psychology, and
feline birth signs.*

NAMES AND NAMING

"The Naming of Cats is a difficult matter," wrote T.
Eliot in *Old Possum's Book of Practical Cats*. He didn
make it any easier by suggesting that cats should hav
"three different names": one "the family use daily",
one that's "more dignified", and one known only to
the cat, a "deep and inscrutable, singular Name".
Here are some suggestions specially chosen to suit a
cat of Oriental origin.

ASIA *The continent that gave birth to the Siamese cat.*

CAPPUCCINO *For a creamy white Seal-point Siamese cat with markings of darkest, richest coffee.*

CORIANDER *A fragrant herb, much used in Thai cookery.*

CRYSTAL *After the nineteenth-century Crystal Palace Cat Show where the Siamese cat was first seen in public.*

GALANGAL *A ginger-like spice, common in Thailand, and used to give fire and flavour to many dishes.*

JEMMA *One of the first Siamese to come to Europe. Jemma was a male, but Gemma would be a suitable female name.*

LAPIS *The brilliant blue gemstone, lapis lazuli, has the same intense colour as the eyes of a Siamese cat.*

PAVAROTTI *For a Siamese who likes to exercise his vocal cords loudly, melodiously, and in front of an admiring audience.*

PYEWACKET *A Siamese witches' cat, who featured in the play* ll, Book and Candle *by John van Druten.*

RAJAH *The original Burmese cats who guarded Buddhist temples* Burma *in the fifteenth century were known as Rajahs.*

RANGOON *Capital of Burma, a city full of exotic atmosphere.*

RUSSELL *After Major Gordon Russell, recipient of a pair of* irmans *given to him by Tibetan priests in 1919.*

SUNNY *For a cat who thinks the whole world revolves around him.*

SUSIE *Short for Susie Wong, the beautiful half-Burmese star of* ul Osborn's *play of the same name.*

SUN *In honour of Tsun Kyan-kse, the blue-eyed Burmese* ddess *whose temple was patrolled by Birman cats.*

UNDERSTANDING YOUR SIAMESE

Does your cat have any difficult personality quirks
that you find hard to handle? Here are the knottier
parts of the Siamese psyche, unravelled.

ATTENTION ON DEMAND

My *two-year-old Siamese,
Wong, expects immediate
attention whenever he
demands it. He yowls for food
and cuddles, and shouts even
louder if he wants to go in or
out. And if we don't obey
instantly, he sprays us.*

🐾 Wong is obviously a
particularly clever Siamese, and
has worked out exactly how to
get his own way. One glance at
his quivering tail-tip has you
running to pander to his
whims, rather than face the
consequences. What you have
to do is get the upper hand, by
ignoring Wong's demands and
giving him attention when it
suits you. You'll have to put up
with his furious spraying for a
day or two, but fortunately this
cat is clever enough to learn a
new pattern of behaviour once
he realises that his old tricks
don't work any more.

SCAREDY CAT

*Thistledown is my affectionate
Birman who has suddenly becom
terrified of strangers. When the
doorbell rings she hides under
the bed and won't come out unt
the coast is clear.*

🐾 Has Thistledown been scare
by a noisy or insensitive guest
recently? If so, she is probably
obeying her survival instinct i
avoiding any new threat. To
regain her confidence, put her
into her travelling basket, and
place it in the room where you
entertain guests before they
arrive so she can't
run away. To reassure her,
visitors should come
into the room
accompanied by
someone familiar
to Thistledown.
Ask strangers
not to approach
the cat, but to
sit down

ietly some distance from the
sket. Repeat this procedure
henever you have guests, and
adually Thistledown will
arn that visitors do not pose a
reat. However, it may be
me time before she
mpletely gets over her fear.

Hypersensitive

aisie, my Siamese, adores being
roked – except on her tummy. If
ry to tickle her there, she often
tes and leaps out of my arms.

Deep Thinker

l cats have their foibles –
amese more than most.

Cats seem to be able to go
into a state of blissful, baby-
like relaxation when they are
being stroked and cuddled, but
many cats dislike being
touched on their sensitive
abdomen and hind legs. Then
they suddenly feel vulnerable
and trapped, and respond with
their best self-defence
mechanism – their teeth and
claws. The simple answer is to
avoid stroking your cat's more
ticklish areas.

CAT BIRTH SIGNS

Find out all about your cat's Chinese birth sign.

THE SIGN OF THE GOAT

15 February 1991 – 3 February 1992
& 28 January 1979 – 15 February 1980

The Goat is a sign of great charm and cats born under its influence will endear themselves to their owners and everyone they meet. Although shy at heart, these cats sparkle in front of an audience.

THE SIGN OF THE HORSE

27 February 1990 – 14 February 1991
& 7 February 1978 – 27 January 1979

Suave and elegant, cats born in the year of the Horse are highly aristocratic creatures. Intelligent and quick learners, these cats love

being the centre of attention, and are sometimes very excitab

THE SIGN OF THE SNAKE

6 February 1989 – 26 January 1990
& 18 February 1977 – 6 February 197

Snake cats are renowned for thei grace and good looks. They have tendency to indulge in frantic bursts of activity, but there is als

a more reserved side to their character. Solitary by nature, they spend long hours sitting quietly and thinking by themselves.

The Sign of the Dragon

17 February 1988 – 5 February 1989
& 31 January 1976 – 17 February 1977

Highly intelligent, Dragon cats are quick to seize opportunities and never miss a trick. Born lucky, they are outgoing and energetic lines. Cats of this sign are often arrogant and flamboyant.

The Sign of the Cat

29 January 1987 – 16 February 1988

What soothing companions these cats are. They are often home-loving, and warmth and comfort are vital to their happiness. Well-mannered, they take particular pride over their appearance and are always beautifully groomed.

The Sign of the Tiger

9 February 1986 – 28 January 1987

Impulsive and brave, cats born under this lucky sign tend to act first and think later, which can get them into trouble. The owner of a Tiger cat needs to be very watchful, as these energetic and extrovert creatures love exploring and their adventurous spirit often leads them far from home.

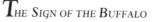

The Sign of the Buffalo

20 February 1985 – 8 February 1986

This sign can be inscrutable in t.
best Siamese tradition. Althougl
they may sometimes appear aloof
Buffalo cats are shy and often wa
of strangers. It is impossible to
read their thoughts and they won't encourage you to try.

The Sign of the Rat

2 February 1984 – 19 February 1985

If anything interesting is going on,
a cat born under the sign of the
Rat will be in the midst of it.
Curious and gregarious, these cats
usually lead eventful lives. They

adore their owners and will do almost anything to please the

The Sign of the Pig

13 February 1983 – 1 February 1984

Extremely vocal, with a wide
repertoire of sounds, cats born
under the sign of the Pig make
sure that they are understood.
Peacemakers, who hate the soun.
of arguments, they will intervene to try and cool heated tempers
They are lovers of luxury and have expensive tastes in food.

The Sign of the Dog

25 January 1982 – 12 February 1983

Alert and interested, cats born under this sign will follow you around everywhere to see what you are doing. They tend to dislike being left alone and prefer human company. Moodiness can be a problem with these felines.

The Sign of the Rooster

5 February 1981 – 24 January 1982

Rooster cats are very volatile and sometimes behave impetuously. The rest of the time they wear a dignified air and stroll around, tail erect, with great pride. Although they are devoted to their owners, they can be very self-centred.

The Sign of the Monkey

16 February 1980 – 4 February 1981

It's easy to be taken in by the Monkey cat's delightful personality, but cats born under this sign can be devious. They are clever at getting themselves out of tight corners and know how to assume an air of innocence. These cats are easily bored, perhaps because they are so intelligent.

PAMPERED
Cat

*All the devoted owner
needs to know about the
care and cosseting of
Siamese cats.*

CHOOSING A KITTEN

It can be so hard to decide which is the kitten
for you, that you'll want them all.

*P*URE *WHITE KITTENS*
Siamese kittens are
often smaller at birth
than other breeds. When
born, the kittens are pure
white. The gene that
produces the "points" on the
face, paws, and tail is
sensitive to heat and the
markings appear gradually
on the cooler parts of the
body. Although kittens
are usually born blind,
the sapphire-blue eyes of
the Siamese are sometimes
half-open when the kittens
are born, and open fully
shortly afterwards.

*S*HOW *KITTENS*
If you plan to show your cat, buy
from a reputable breeder and ask for
full documentation of the pedigree.

WHICH KITTEN?

When you visit a litter to make your choice, watch the kittens at play for a while.

Choose one that is pert and lively, with lots of energy and an inquisitive nature.

Make sure that the kitten runs and jumps easily.

Look for bright eyes and clean nose and ears.

Open the mouth and check that the teeth and gums are sound and healthy.

Look through the fur for any signs of fleas.

Siamese cats adore human companionship, so don't choose one unless you can return the love that your pet will give.

KEEPING WARM

When you take your kitten home, let him settle in completely before allowing him to explore outside.

LITTER MATES

Two kittens are twice as much fun as one, and will be happy companions.

49

CAT GLAMOUR

Most Siamese-type cats have short hair, which make
grooming straightforward. However, if you own a
longhaired variety such as a Colourpoint or Balinese
you will need to groom your pet every day to prevent
the thick coat from becoming tangled or matted.

*N*O MORE TANGLES
*Longhaired cats should be gently
brushed and combed every day.*

*T*IPS FOR GROOMING

1 *Rub grooming powder
into the coat, making sure
that it is evenly distributed.*

2 *Brush through the fur,
dealing with any tangles
that you come across.*

FELINE FACIALS

Clean the ears gently with a cotton-wool bud and wipe carefully around the eyes with a moistened pad of cotton wool.

TOOTH CARE

The teeth can be cleaned to prevent a build-up of tartar. Use a soft toothbrush with either a solution of salt water or feline toothpaste available from pet shops.

Finish with an all-over brush, using long, sweeping strokes down the whole body.

4 For extra gloss, rub the coat gently with a piece of velvet, silk, or chamois.

EXOTIC CUISINE

Although cats should not be given highly spiced food
many of them do enjoy well-flavoured dishes. Here a
some gastronomic goodies guaranteed to tempt the
most selective feline appetite on those special days
when you want to lavish a little extra affection on
your cat. Allow food to cool before serving.

Chicken Stir Fry

*Dice raw chicken breast. Heat
oil in a wok or frying pan, and
cook the meat quickly over a
high flame, stirring all of the
time. When the chicken is
almost cooked, stir in a few
flaked almonds for added
crunch. Allow to cool
and serve with a
little plain
boiled rice.*

Aromatic Fi

*Place fillets of whiting or coley
a foil parcel. Pour over a li
milk, season, and sprinkle w
finely chopped coriander. Ba
in the oven for 20 minutes
a medium heat. When cooke
flake, removing bones, a
serve with the cooki
liquid poured ov
Garnish w
coriand*

PRAWN TEMPTATION

...x cooked prawns with plain
...gurt and pile on to squares of
...sted wholemeal bread.

OEUF ROYALE

Lightly scramble an egg beaten
with a tablespoon of milk, and
stir in slivers of smoked salmon.

STEAK TARTARE

...esh steak or mince, very
...ely chopped and served raw,
...ll make your cat's eyes light
... . Raw meat should only be
...en as an occasional treat.

CHICKEN LIVER RISOTTO

Cook chopped chicken liver for
about ten minutes in a well-
flavoured stock. Stir into plain
boiled rice and serve sprinkled
with chopped mint or parsley.

SALMON DELIGHT

...move the bones from
...nned salmon
...d mix with
...ked pasta.
...rinkle
...ese on
... top and
...lt under
... grill. Cool
...ore serving.

FRESH FRUIT PARFAIT

Siamese cats are often
partial to fresh
fruit. For this
dessert, put
two table-
spoons of
plain yogurt
in a bowl. Top
with tangerine
or slices of apple.

My Cat's Personal Record

Name ...... Leah   Wilson ......

Pedigree name ......

Sex ...... female ......

Date of birth ......

Breed ...... seal point Siamese ......

Colour of eyes ...... Blue ......

Description of markings ...... Chocolate point

Name and breed of mother ......

......

Name and breed of father ......

......

Name and address of breeder ......

......

......

Cat show prizes ......

......

...ods favoured ..... KIT KAT ....

...ods frowned on ....

...vourite drink ..... Water ....

...est possible treat ....

...ocabulary (list sounds and meanings) ....

....

....

...dy language (describe movements and meanings) ....

....

....

...tention-seeking ploys ....

....

...t tricks and games ....

....

...ost precarious perch ....

...eferred snoozing places ....

...ecial stroking zones ....

....

55

A-Z OF SIAMESE CATS

A IS FOR
AFFECTIONATE
Siamese cats often
form a devoted
attachment to those
who care for them.

B IS FOR BREEDING
If you want to breed
pedigree kittens
from your Siamese
cat, consult a
professional breeder.
A Siamese crossed
with a non-Siamese
can also produce
beautiful and very
sturdy kittens.

E IS FOR ELEGANCE
Long, slender legs
and a very svelte
bodyline give
the Siamese
an elegant
look.

C IS FOR COAT
The close, smooth
coat benefits from
daily combing,
which removes any
dead hairs and keeps
the fur immaculate.

D IS FOR DELICATE
Although it is a
myth that Siamese
are a delicate breed,
they do love comfort
and need a warm
basket and plenty of
good food.

F IS FOR FOREIGN
SHORTHAIR
The name given to
shorthaired cat bre
from a Siamese
crossed with other
types. Foreign
Shorthairs come in
a wide variety of
different colours.

G IS FOR GENES
In the past, careles
breeding has
produced weak
kittens with faded
markings. Stricter
control has resolve
the problem.

H IS FOR HEAT
There's no mistakir
a female Siamese o
heat. The breed is
renowned for its
strident mating call
and restless
behaviour, which
can go on for sever
days at a time.

IS FOR
NTELLIGENCE
any Siamese cats
e exceptionally
right and can solve
roblems with
onsiderable skill
nd dexterity. They
e sometimes
illing to learn
icks, although they
ill usually only
erform when it suits
em. Some city
wners have even
anaged to train
eir Siamese cats to
alk on a lead.

IS FOR JEALOUSY
erhaps because a
iamese becomes so
tached to his
wner, he also tends
resent the
trusion of other
ets and, sometimes,
her humans.
owever, if
troduced when
ry young, Siamese
ts can become
od friends with
her animals.

K IS FOR KITTENS

Although small at
birth, Siamese
kittens soon develop
a healthy appetite.
Start them on solids
when they are about
four weeks old.

L IS FOR LOSING

Nothing is more
distressing than the
loss of a much-loved
pet. Never let your
cat stay out all night
as this is when
accidents tend to
happen. Give an
early evening feed to
lure night-loving
cats indoors. Once
inside, shut the cat
flap firmly.

M IS FOR MOTHERHOOD

Although Siamese
cats do make
excellent and
loving mothers,
they sometimes
need help at the
time of the birth.
For some reason, the
breed doesn't always
know how to deal
with new-born
kittens. Consult
your vet about this
if your cat is about
to produce a litter.
The vet should also
be notified of the
likely date of the
kittens' arrival so
that he can be on
hand in case there
are complications.

N IS FOR NEUTERING

Unless you are planning to show or breed from your cat, it is kindest to have him or her neutered at between four and six months old.

O IS FOR OLD AGE

Fifteen or sixteen years is a good average age for a Siamese. An older cat will eat less and sleep more than a younger animal, and will appreciate a warm bed in a draught-free spot.

P IS FOR POINTS

The name given to the typical Siamese markings on face, paws, and tail. There are lots of possible colours, including seal, lilac, tabby, blue, and cream.

Q IS FOR QUICK WITS

The canny Siamese is always quick to spot an opportunity for extra food or a comfy bed. They are also good at outwitting their owners and are extremely clever at getting into places where they shouldn't be.

R IS FOR REGISTRATION

Registering the details of name, colour, and parents is a must for pedigree kittens, and should be done when they are around five weeks old. Register all kittens with the governing body, who must also be notified about any change of ownership. Take advice on this from your breeder.

S IS FOR SHOWING

The attention-loving Siamese has good temperament for showing. On the day of the show, the cat must be healthy, perfectly groomed, and allowed plenty of time to settle down in his pen before judging. Get your pet used to being handled by strangers before the show to avoid any sign of nervousness during judging.

T IS FOR TEETH

Brush teeth gently with a soft toothbrush and salt water solution to prevent a build-up of damaging tartar. The breath should be pleasant and the gums firm and pink. If you suspect a rotten or painful tooth, take your cat to the vet for its extraction.

U IS FOR UNDERSTANDING
A Siamese cat is happiest when he has plenty of human companionship and love. He will quickly feel neglected if left alone for long periods, and will go to great lengths to recapture your full attention. Treat your Siamese cat with plenty of care, and he will be your devoted friend for life.

V IS FOR VOICE
One outstanding characteristic of a Siamese is its voice, which is quite unlike that of any other cat. These cats often enjoy "talking" to their owners, answering with a whole range of sounds. Siamese cats can be demanding and their loud howls for attention cannot be ignored for long.

W IS FOR WATER
Don't worry if your Siamese turns up his impeccable nose at a bowl of fresh water and refuses to drink. Cats extract a lot of liquid from their food, and can manage on hardly any water without harm. Make sure that clean water is always available though, just in case your cat suddenly develops a thirst.

X IS FOR XTROVERT
This is not the breed for the cat owner who is looking for a placid pet who sleeps all day by the fire. A Siamese loves nothing more than an admiring audience. Your extrovert pet will keep you entertained with his antics, acrobatics, and mischief.

Y IS FOR YOGURT
A healthy addition to a feline diet. Offer a little of the plain variety for your cat to sample.

Z IS FOR ZEN
An Oriental method of contemplating the inner nature in order to achieve enlightenment.

I N D E X

ACKNOWLEDGMENTS

Key: t=top; b=bottom; c=centre; l=left; r=right

All photography by Jane Burton except for:
Animals Unlimited: 40–41
The Bridgeman Art Library: 10, 11t, 13
Camera Press (photo by Norman Parkinson): 14
E.T. Archive: 11b
Ronald Grant Collection: 15
Images Colour Library: 12
Dave King: 9tr, 17tr, 18tr, 19tr, 19c, 19b, 22–23, 26–27, 28–29, 30b, 31b,
32–33, 34–35, 47tr, 50–51

Design Assistance: Patrizio Semproni, Rachel Griffin, Camilla Fox
Additional Picture Research: Diana Morris
Illustrations: Susan Robertson, Stephen Lings, Clive Spong